Homestead Poetry

Shauna Hyde

BookLeaf Publishing

India | USA | UK

Made with ❤ on the BookLeaf Publishing Platform
www.bookleafpub.in
www.bookleafpub.com

Dedication

To those who teach what matters, prophets in the night,
guide for the soul.

Preface

Poetry has long been the language of cultures throughout time. As we continue to learn and perfect the language, may be we inspired to new translations.

Acknowledgements

Thanks for all I have been taught and am yet to learn.

1. The Garden

The garden I grow depends on me
I can harvest crops or I can harvest weeds
The beauty and the product
are all up to me
What will I dwell on?
What will I see?
What is nurtured is what will grow
So I decide, row by row
The beauty I crave and the garden I sow
Will only be produced by what I feed
Beauty or death
Tangles of root
Knots of vine
Small buds and flowers
Roses in bloom

2. Spices

To add cardamom, nutmeg, cinnamon and spice
Is the heart of the baker
The bread rises
The cakes iced
The pot is stirred
The measures of life
A cup of flour
A spoon to mix
A taste of salt
A pinch of pepper
A splash of wine
The spice of life added over time
The one that is the sweetest
The one that never fails
The one that feeds the most
The one that enhances
Every dish
Every soul
Is none other than love from the baker's soul

3. Favorites

The rays of sun forming beams to earth
The dew on a petal
The trees of girth
The hope of creation
The coming of birth
The flutter of butterfly wings
The shelter from rain
The feather that dances
Caught in a flame

4. Courage

To dwell in the valley always looking up
Surrounded by mountains
Feeling dwarfed and lost
Always seeking new heights and views
Daring to wander what sights might be new
To stay small is easy
To rise is not
To rise requires dropping the weight and all that it costs
Daring to embrace the unknown and feared
Daring to rise when others would add more weight
Stay small
Stay with us
Stay surrounded by mountains unable to rise
Sometimes courage isn't a step
It is a simple daring to cut
The ropes that bind us
The strings that tie
The ribbon that weaves
The lace that lies

5. Change

Feared and unwanted
Unless it is controlled and chosen
Dreaded and needed
Only the adaptable survive
Cha, cha, cha, changes
The revelation ranges
Despair and stubborn
Resistance and acceptance
Transformation and healing
Pruning and weeding
Desert to blooming
Seed to flower

6 . Ruts

Day after day routine
Digs a trench in the soul
Some find it comfort
Some find it dull
Some fight it and scream in the night
Others will it to decrease the fright
Let us hang curtains and plant a row
Ruts define the shape of our souls
Let us push the envelope and open the door
Let us not, we might want more
Ruts; chains and flight
Ruts; comfort and horror
Ruts; home and prison
Ruts; good for the soul
Water follows the rut to bring refreshment
The path of least resistance
Break free to dig a new one
Hang curtains and plant a row

7. Fear

Icy fingers run down the spine
Tingling nerves and fraying edges
Impending doom is a mountainous weight
The shoe hovering
The sonic boom paused
The dawn never rising
The dread that fills the toes
The nerves that shake the knees
The stomach uneased
Fear runs amok among the living
Relentless and unforgiving

8 . Rage

Somewhere along the way rage simply quietly takes
root
The injuries add up
The disappointments abound
The hurts, the slights, always come round
We learn to tap into it to face the hard and cold
We learn that if we stay warm
We can afford to be bold
It relentlessly pulls forward if we don't look back
It can make up the difference for what is lack
It can be a driving force if well contained
It can ruin when unrestrained
To assuage it or fuel it is all that remains
Somewhere along the way, it might be tamed

9. Home

Sea salt, bay leaves, and cloves
Cinnamon, sage, roses, and hope
Chickens and gardens and love
Build fences
Mend barns
Grow peace and strength
Let home descend on your bones
Pies in the oven and cats in laps
A little piece of heaven
That's where home is at

10. Choices Made

You wanted me to go
All secret plots and deceitful throes
You mocked and accused
Blamed and waged war on my soul
With pretend smiles and limpid care
The black bile of your spirit easily flowed
You say you won
You made me go
In truth, I saw my future in your hate and made haste
lest my soul begin to match yours too closely and with
too much waste

11. Innocence

Is it true that innocence is lost?
Does it get taken, snatched away by rude awakening?
Is it the price of understanding, of knowledge gained?
Is it a slow trickle of awareness that caresses our minds,
leading us into new paths?
Is it a downpour, a deluge of powerless thought?
Can it be preserved or is it more at risk when left
unaware?
Endless questions for the price we pay along the way.

12. Hope

Hope is the balloon that takes flight
The bulb that becomes a rose
Hope is the leaving of the night
The turning of a page
Hope is the strength to keep going
Hope is the eternal struggle of letting go and gaining life
It is the babe in spring
The birds that sing
Hope is the whisper in the night that it is not yet done
It is chains unlocked
It is both burden and weightless light
It is the life that thrumbs in our veins
It is the forward motion of relentless gains

13. Love

We love love

The idea, the feeling, the anticipation

The wanting, the longing, the being

The labor of love gets lost in the dreams, the stories, and

the clouds

The work of love in choosing time and again to forgive

To enjoy imperfection

To let go of control

To accept

To partner

To find hope, grace, passion and wonder all in the labor

of love

14. Wander

The poet said, "Take the road less travelled."
What roads are left to take?
Wandering, roaming, gloaming
The patterns of time flow through the ages like sand in
an hourglass constantly flipped over and over
Spinning, whirling, twirling the grains
What is new for the roaming soul?
What is left for the adventurer?
We are destined to arrive at the same roads eternally

15. Time

Time flits by like a darting butterfly
Flower to flower, seamlessly drifting
Bud to wilting
Seed to dying
Time is relentless in its forward march
Never backward
Yet ever repeating
Cocoon to wings
Flitting and flying
Never caught
Yet experienced all the same

16. Grief

The price of love they say is found in the weight we later
bear alone
The memories are so sweet they hurt
The hope of a future lost
The wanting of a past forever gone

My heart slipped out of my body and left rivers down my
face
They are seeking you and the empty space you left
behind
I wonder why when you left you took my heart with
you
Then I remember: That's the price of love

17. Disrespect

The words dropped on my heart like pebbles in water
Plink, plink, plink
A gentle undoing of love
A tear in the fabric of who I am
Words that haunt and trip
Words that flit through edges of all I hold dear
Plink, plink, plink
Is the sound of undoing

18. Loneliness

The days are full of memories and heartache
In the hour before dawn, I am weighed down
Awakened by what went wrong
By what could have gone right
If only, you had been kind

19. Snow Days

I watch the snow fall and silence falls with it
The warmth of blanket and cat nourish my soul
The stillness is a balm that mends the edges of what
busy-ness tore apart

20. Brokenness

They say that we are all broken
They say that is how the light gets in
They say our life's work is to seek healing
But
What if being broken means we are actually whole
again?

21. The Void

We try to fill the spot that's hollow
It sits somewhere inside
It's gaping mouth begging like a bird in the nest, "Feed
me."
We run to parties, work til we hate our jobs
We drink and smoke and fill up on dope
We place orders and shop before anything new hits the
floor
We run through people and money and still want more
The Void controls us and wants more still
Screen time, mean time, gossip time, vent time
Feeding time, snack time, fast food time
We want and want and want some more
Always with one eye on the door
We beg for validation, affirmation, and need to be the
loved
The most special, the smartest, the rarest, the most, the
most
The Void won't stop until we stop it
The Void won't stop until we control it

When we choose the right food, the gaping mouth
closes
When we choose peace, love, joy, and hope.....The Void is
at last finally sated